CHRISTIAN MISSIONARY
ALLIANCE CHURCH
853 S. Main Street
Homer City, Pa. 15748

When Our Church Building Burned Down

When Our Church Building Burned Down

Martha Whitmore Hickman

Illustrated by
SANDRA SPEIDEL

Abingdon Press
Nashville

WHEN OUR CHURCH BUILDING BURNED DOWN

Copyright © 1986 by Martha Whitmore Hickman
Art copyright © 1986 by Sandra Speidel

All Rights Reserved

Library of Congress Cataloging in Publication Data

Hickman, Martha Whitmore, 1925–
   When our church building burned down.
   Summary: When his neighborhood church burns down, a young boy learns that the church is the people, not the building.
   [1. Church—Fiction. 2. Fire—Fiction] I. Title.
PZ7.H 53143Wm 1986   [E]   85-13504
ISBN 0-687-45023-3 (alk. paper)

This book is printed on acid-free paper.

Words on pages 23 and 48 from "I Am the Church" by Richard Avery. Copyright © 1972 by Hope Publishing Co., Carol Stream, IL 60187. All rights reserved. Used by permission.

Manufactured in the United States of America

To Hoyt

One Saturday morning I was sitting on my porch when I heard a fire siren. The sound seemed to be coming down Center Street. I looked over toward the corner.

Whoosh! A fire engine went by. The siren shrieked and wailed.

Another engine went by. And another.

That must be a big fire, I thought.

Then I noticed something. The sirens stopped soon after they passed the corner.

My father came out on the porch. He was holding the newspaper. "Sounds close," he said.

"I know it," I said.

"Sounds like it's near our church," he said.

Our church is on Center Street—just two blocks away. We walk unless it's raining or snowing.

"I sure hope not," I said.

"You want to walk over?" he said. He put the paper down on the porch swing. He opened the screen door and called to my mother, "Sammy and I are going over to Center Street, to see what's going on."

We hurried down the street. We saw other people going in the same direction.

Three houses down, Mr. Hawkins came out of his house. "What do you think it is?" he asked as he joined us. Elizabeth came hurrying after him. "Wait, Dad!"

We waited while she caught up. Elizabeth is in my Sunday school class.

"I hope it's not our church," I said.

"Me, too," she said.

"Look at the smoke, Jack," Mr. Hawkins said to my father. Down at the corner black smoke blew above the street. "Windy, too," Mr. Hawkins said. "Not good." I pulled my jacket around me.

We got to the corner. For a minute we stopped, just standing there, looking.

"Oh, no!" Mr. Hawkins said.

"It *is* the church!" my father said.

"Our church!" I said. I held my father's hand tighter, and he held mine.

"Oh, no!" Elizabeth said.

We hurried toward the church. Fire engines were parked in the middle of the street. Firefighters scampered up and down ladders.

People were standing, watching—staying out of the firefighters' way. Hoses were all over the street, and barriers, to keep anyone from getting too close.

We found a place near one of the barriers. Flames were coming out the upstairs windows. Firefighters sprayed water in the windows. Smoke blew everywhere.

I was standing next to Elizabeth. "That's our Sunday school room!" I said. "On that side is our Sunday school room!"

She looked worried. "Oh, no!" she said.

I looked up at my father. "Is anybody in the church?" I asked.

"I don't know. Dave Baxter's usually there Saturday mornings."

Mr. Baxter is our minister. He plays and sings with us and tells us stories. Sometimes when he drives the church bus he drives by a farm and makes noises like the animals.

"And Mr. Curtis, too," Elizabeth said.

Mr. Curtis is the custodian. He carved a pumpkin for our Halloween party.

The church doors opened. Out came firefighters, and two other men in regular clothes. They were all carrying things.

"There are Dave and Mr. Curtis!" my father said.

They were carrying books. The firefighters were carrying chairs and tables and other big things.

A man in the crowd called out, "They're bringing out the pulpit!"

Someone else called, "Get the pulpit Bible!"

Other people called out:

"The Memorial Gifts Book!"

"The big cross!"

"The embroidered altar cloths!"

"The new hymnbooks!"

Suddenly I remembered something. I shouted out: "Get the costumes! In the dress-up corner. For the Lost Sheep!"

Elizabeth looked at me. She wrinkled her nose. "What?" she said.

"We're doing the parable!" I said. "For the congregation this time! It's my turn to be the Lost Sheep and wear the sheep costume!"

She nodded. "I forgot." She leaned over the barrier. "Get the sheep costume!" she shouted to the firefighters. "It looks like a sheep!" To me she said, "It's only somebody's old white jacket with black button eyes." She turned back to the firefighters. "Save the sheep costume!" she called again.

It was no use. The firefighters shook their heads. "Can't go back in," one of them called. They held the big hoses and pumped streams of water at the building.

We stood and watched while the roof fell in and the steeple tumbled over and the building burned.

We were all very sad.

People started to leave.

Mr. Hawkins and Elizabeth and my father and I began to walk home. "I wonder how it started," Mr. Hawkins said.

"I don't know," my father said.

Elizabeth and I didn't say anything. I was thinking of all my favorite places in the church—the little closet where we put our coats and boots, the table in the library with the blue and yellow chairs, the tower room the big kids fixed up with curtains and pictures of the ocean. And the sanctuary, where the light from the window showed rainbow colors on my mother's ring when I sat beside her waiting for the prayer to be finished.

When we got home we told my mother about the fire. She shook her head. "Oh, my!" She was crying.

"What will we do without our church?" I asked. "Will we build a new one? How long will it take?" I didn't say anything about the Lost Sheep.

"Probably we'll build a new building," my father said. "I don't know how long it will take. The building's gone. But we still have a church. The church is really the people who go there."

"Like that song," my mother reminded me: "I am the church, You are the church, We are the church together . . ."

"But how can you have a church if you don't have a building to put it in?" I said.

"You can have a family, can't you—if you don't have a house to put it in?" my mother said.

I thought about that. "Sure. I guess," I said.

"If our house burned down we'd still be a family, right?" my father said.

"Right!" I laughed out loud. I was beginning to feel a little better about the church. "But we'd have to live somewhere else," I said. "Where's the church going to live?"

"We'll find a place," my father said.

Just then the telephone rang. My mother went to answer it. When she came back she was smiling. "Well, that's the answer to our question. That was Margaret Patrella calling for the telephone chain. We won't have Sunday school this week, but church tomorrow will meet at 10:30 in O'Shanahan's Restaurant. It's closed on Sundays, and they've invited us to use their building. Isn't that nice?"

"Sure is," my father said. He stood up. "Let's call the people on our list," he said. He and my mother went toward the kitchen.

O'Shanahan's Restaurant! I thought. It sure was funny to think of church in a restaurant. It wouldn't be the same at all—no library, no tower room, no sanctuary to sit in and be quiet, or sing, or do our dramatization of the parable about finding the lost sheep.

Sunday morning came. We got up and had our breakfast. We got dressed for church. We started down the street—to O'Shanahan's Restaurant.

As we went past the Hawkins' house, Elizabeth and her big sister, Ann, and their mother and father came out.

We all got to the corner. There, in the next block, on the other side of the road, was a big heap of stones and ashes. Slowly, we walked along toward it. When we got across from it we stopped. "That's sad," Mrs. Hawkins said.

"Really sad," my mother said.

We waited a few minutes, looking at it quietly. Then we went on.

One block farther down the street, we came to O'Shanahan's Restaurant. People were going in. We'd been there lots of times before. But never to church!

We pushed the revolving door. Inside, there was Mr. O'Shanahan, smiling. "Welcome. Good morning," he said.

The restaurant looked strange. The tables were pushed to one side of the room, next to a row of booths. The orange chairs were lined up in rows. In front was a long table with a white cloth on it. On the table were a bouquet of flowers, a cross, and a big book.

I poked my father. "Is that our church's big Bible?" I asked.

"I think so," he whispered. "I think Dave rescued it. The Presbyterians loaned us the cross from their chapel."

More people came in. They sat down in the orange chairs and talked softly to one another.

Our minister walked up to the front. He wasn't wearing his robe. I wondered if it got burned in the fire.

He turned around and stood in front of all of us. "Good morning!" he said, and smiled. "The Lord be with you!"

"And also with you!" the people said.

"We don't have our hymnbooks today, so we're going to sing hymns we know. The choir here is going to help us." He waved toward the front of the restaurant, and two rows of people stood up from their orange chairs.

"We'll start with 'Holy, Holy, Holy, Lord God Almighty,' " he said. "Let's all stand." He lifted his hands, and the rows of chairs screeched and bumped. We all stood up and began to sing. I sang as much as I knew. "Holy, holy, holy," I sang; "Lord God Almighty." I listened for the rest: "Early in the morning our song shall rise to Thee." I felt my hair tingle at the back of my neck. This almost felt like church.

Just then I saw my Sunday school teacher, Mrs. Allen, at the end of the row. She was beckoning to Elizabeth and me. We squeezed past our parents and followed her to one of the booths at the side of the restaurant.

"Wait here," she said. "I'll get the others."

There on the orange table of the booth was a big box, with what looked like a white T-shirt sticking out.

Mrs. Allen came back with Nathan, Jenny, Marie and Luke. She began pulling things from the box—T-shirts and a bathrobe. Underneath the box was a cane—just like we used to have in our dress-up corner! She whispered, "Sorry I was a little late getting here. I was collecting these things. So we can do our parable."

We all looked at each other, surprised. "The fire?" I said. "I thought the dress-up things all burned."

"They did," she whispered. "But I got some others. The story's the important thing." She rummaged in the box of clothes. "We have to hurry," she said. "We come soon after this hymn. Now, Sammy . . ."

She pulled something white and furry out of the box and held it up to me. "Most of the sheep will just wear the T-shirts," she said. "But you, Sammy, get to wear this bathmat!"

"A bathmat!" I said. She put her fingers to her lips. "It's softer than that old white jacket, anyway," she whispered. "Sorry I didn't have time to sew on buttons for eyes. But here"—she held up two black belts—"to fasten it on you," she explained.

The bathmat was soft and cozy. I held it around me while Mrs. Allen fastened one belt around my shoulders, and another around my waist. The other sheep were putting on their T-shirts, and Jenny, who was the shepherd, was tying the belt around the bathrobe.

"Where shall we graze?" Marie asked. "We were supposed to graze near the choir."

"Oh, just around the front of the restaurant," Mrs. Allen said.

"Where shall I get lost?" I said. "I was supposed to get lost behind the pulpit."

"You could get under one of the orange chairs," she said.

We were ready to go. Just then the minister looked over and said, "The children are going to dramatize one of our scriptures this morning."

Out we went—I in my belted-on bathmat, the other sheep in their T-shirts, and Jenny in the bathrobe and holding the cane. We wandered around the front of the restaurant, and I got under one of the orange chairs. Along came Jenny, gathering in the sheep one by one. She pretended she didn't see me. From under the chair I could see Mr. O'Shanahan, looking surprised.

"Where's that other sheep?" Jenny held her hand over her eyes, looking all around the restaurant.

At first I was quiet. Then, when I thought it was time, I bleated.

Jenny rushed over. She touched the furry bathmat with her cane and said, "Here's the other sheep—the one that was lost. Hurray!"

Then all the sheep stood up and clapped and all the people in the rows of orange chairs clapped, too.

I looked around. It wasn't our usual sanctuary, but it felt like church to me—everyone looking at one another, everyone looking happy and proud. Even though our building burned.

"Thank you very much, boys and girls," Mr. Baxter said. "That was wonderful." He looked back to Mr. O'Shanahan, who was standing behind the last row of chairs. "That was the parable of the Lost Sheep, Mr. O'Shanahan."

Mr. O'Shanahan nodded. "I guessed it was something like that," he called. "I know most of those parable stories myself."

We all started to follow Mrs. Allen toward the booth to take off our T-shirts and bathrobe and bathmat. But before we went she held her hand up and said, loud enough for everyone to hear, "Mr. O'Shanahan could be the Good Samaritan

in the Good Samaritan parable. When we were in trouble he helped us out."

"That's right," Mr. Baxter said, and all the people clapped for Mr. O'Shanahan, too.

"Now let's sing another song," Mr. Baxter said. "It's an especially good song for today, when our church building has burned down. I think the children can lead us in this one." He turned to us. "If the Lost Sheep parable players will wait just another minute. . .

"I am the church," he started, and everyone joined in:

"You are the church!
We are the church together!
All who follow Jesus,
All around the world!
Yes we're the church together."

Then we went to the booth to take off our costumes.